Disney's TOONTOWN

Old MacDonald Has a Farm

Illustrated by Franc Mateu and Robbin Cuddy

MERRIGOLD PRESS • NEW YORK

Old MacDonald has a farm,

E-I-E-I-O!

And on that farm he has a hen,

With a cluck, cluck here,
And a cluck, cluck there.
Here a cluck, there a cluck,
Everywhere a cluck, cluck.
Old MacDonald has a farm,

E-I-E-I-O!

And on that farm he has a duck,

E-I-E-I-O!

With a quack, quack here,
And a quack, quack there.
Here a quack, there a quack,
Everywhere a quack, quack.
Old MacDonald has a farm,

E-I-E-I-O!

And on that farm he has a pig,

With an oink, oink here,
And an oink, oink there.
Here an oink, there an oink,
Everywhere an oink, oink.
Old MacDonald has a farm,

And on that farm he has a lamb,

With a baa, baa here,
And a baa, baa there.
Here a baa, there a baa,
Everywhere a baa, baa.
Old MacDonald has a farm,

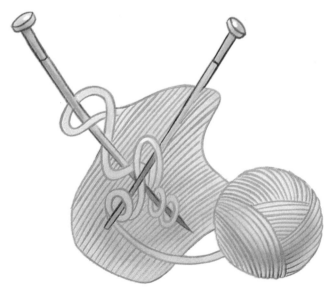

And on that farm he has a cow,

E-I-E-I-O!

With a moo, moo here,
And a moo, moo there.
Here a moo, there a moo,
Everywhere a moo, moo.
Old MacDonald has a farm,

E-I-E-I-O!

And on that farm he has a horse,

With a neigh, neigh here,
And a neigh, neigh there.
Here a neigh, there a neigh,
Everywhere a neigh, neigh.
Old MacDonald has a farm,

E-I-E-I-O!

And on that farm he has a dog,
E-I-E-I-O!

With a woof, woof here,
And a woof, woof there.
Here a woof, there a woof,
Everywhere a woof, woof.
Old MacDonald has a farm,
E-I-E-I-O!

And on that farm he has a cat,

E-I-E-I-O!

With a meow, meow here,
And a meow, meow there.
Here a meow, there a meow,
Everywhere a meow, meow.
Old MacDonald has a farm,

E-I-E-I-O!

And on that farm he has a mouse,

E-I-E-I-O!

With a squeak, squeak here,
And a squeak, squeak there.
Here a squeak, there a squeak,
Everywhere a squeak, squeak.
Old MacDonald has a farm,

E-I-E-I-O!

And on that farm he has a bull,

E-I-E-I-O!

With a snort, snort here,
And a snort, snort there.
Here a snort, there a snort,
Everywhere a snort, snort.
Old MacDonald has a farm,

E-I-E-I-O!

Old MacDonald HAD a farm,

E-I-E-I-O!